Encouraging Your Husband

A Practical Guide to Encourage Your Husband

ILYNMW Publishing
Atlanta Georgia

Dedication

This book is dedicated to my Bride and the love of my life - Debbie.   She is the one who encourages me on a consistent basis.

TFSY

ILYNMW

YAMBFES

Other Books by Paul Beersdorf

- Flowers on Tuesday

- 52 Things I Wish My Father Had Taught Me About Marriage & Family

- The 100 Most Important Words

- Encouraging Your Wife

Contents

Acknowledgements

I want to thank all of our family and friends who helped contribute content to this book.   My Bride is especially good at encouraging me and she has a real knack for knowing just what to say and when to say it. I love her so very much and appreciate the friendship, love and support that she gives me.

Introduction

What is encouragement? Here is a clinical definition:

Definition - Encouragement - something that makes someone more determined, hopeful, or confident

What are some other words for encouragement?

Reassurance
Inspiration
Praise
Reinforcement
Boost
Support

These are all great words!   All of these words should be evident in your life as you strive to encourage your husband.

The goal of this book is to help women to become encouraging "machines" For some women; this is already second nature. They encourage their husband on a regular basis and build him up as a husband, father, son and friend

However, some of you may need a 'nudge" and learn how to better encourage your husband.   This book will provide you some creative and practical resources and guides to help you encourage your husband. You must become a student of your husband and never stop studying him and learning about him and his needs, wants and desires.

Below are some great verses that describe how blessed husbands are to have their Bride.   God knew that husbands needed someone to walk through this life with and he graciously provided you as an incredible companion.

Genesis 2:18
The LORD God said, "It is not good for the man to be alone. I will make a helper suitable for him."

Proverbs 18: 22
He who finds a wife finds a good thing and obtains favor from the LORD.

Proverbs 31:10
An excellent wife, who can find? For her worth is far above jewels.

Proverbs 19:14
House and wealth are an inheritance from fathers, but a prudent wife is from the LORD.

Proverbs 12:4
An excellent wife is the crown of her husband,

Mark 10:9
 What therefore God has joined together let no man separate."

Bring Your "A" Game

What does it mean to bring your "A" game? It means that your husband does not get the "left overs" of your time, talents and treasures. It means that he is not the second or third thought you have for the day, but the first thought you have for the day.

Remember when you were first dating? You could not wait to spend time with him. You anticipated going out on the date and the activities you would enjoy.

He was constantly on your heart and mind. You cleaned up, you dressed up, and you showed up on time! You held his hand. When he walked into room you smiled and your heart leapt.

In other words, you were prepared, thoughtful, considerate and kind. You brought your "A" game when he was pursuing you and he was the target of your affections.

He needs, wants and desires for you to bring your "A" game every day. He wants you to want him! Whether you are a newlywed or have been married for over 20 years, it is your responsibility to continue to make him feel different, better and special.

You can do this through continuous encouragement and thoughtfulness. It will take some work and investment, but mostly you just need to be intentional about making him a priority in your life.

By the way - he is so worth it!!

Communicating With Your Husband

Encouraging your husband is all about making a positive investment in him. One of the primary means of encouraging your husband will be how you communicate with him on a daily basis. Note that I said "daily basis". You should be communicating with your husband each and every day!

What do I mean by communication?

- Verbal - what you say
- Non-verbal - your actions and gestures/facial expressions
- Text
- E-mail
- Snail mail
- Notes
- Social Media posts (Facebook, Twitter, etc.)
- Video conference
- Smoke Signals
- Telegram
- Semaphore flags

Positive communication is one of the keys to a great relationship and a key building block for a long term future together. In the following chapters, you will read;

- Things he needs to see you do when you are communicating with him

- Things he needs to hear you say

- Things he needs to read (from you)

It is your job to become a "communications expert" in regards to your husband. He deserves your very best effort each and every day. It will not be easy, but it is a task worthy of a real woman.

Communication Skills
Things he needs to see you doing when you communicate with him.

When you are communicating with your husband your actions can be just as important as the words you are using. Here are some suggested actions to consider when communicating with your husband.

- Put away your cell phone and focus on him

- Look at him when you are talking and smile

- Turn off the TV (do not just put it on mute)

- Listen without solving (this is tough, but train yourself to just listen). Ask specific questions!

- Do not look at your watch, fidget, or act disinterested in his story (pay attention)

- Praise him in public

- Stop multitasking and focus on him

- Praise him even when he is not around (yes I know he cannot see you doing this, but it is an intentional action on your part and a conscience effort to always be positive about your husband)

- Take his side in arguments with kids, family and friends

- If you are running early or late let him know

- Pay attention to the way he looks

- If you cannot sympathize then empathize.

- Be that shoulder he can lean on

- Make him a priority! He will know this by the amount of time and energy you focus on him.

- When in doubt, ask your husband how you can do a better job communicating with him.

It is just not good enough for you to say that you are not good at communicating. Communication is a skill that can be learned, honed and perfected by anyone who is willing to put in the time, energy and effort to be a better communicator.

The Things he Needs to Hear You Say

Your husband needs to hear you offer encouraging words all the time. According to Harvard Business Review, the highest performing teams in business offer positive comments almost six times more than they offer negative comments.

Interestingly enough, Dr. John Gottman has studied married couples and he suggests that the best ratio of positive to negative comments is 5 to 1.

No matter the source, the idea is that you should be praising and encouraging your husband much more than you are offering criticism.

 Below are over 100 suggested things you can say to your husband if you want to encourage him.   These are not in any particular order; this is a list that my Bride and I compiled, along with the help from some of our friends and family.

Commit today to using these phrases on a frequent basis with your husband.

Below are the different sections that will be covered in this chapter:

- Encouragement When he is Hurting
- Encouraging his Physical Attributes
- Encouragement For Him as a Father
- Encouragement for Him as Your Husband
- Spiritual Encouragement for Him
- General Encouragement For Him
- Encouragement by Time Together
- Encouragement When He is Tired
- Encouragement For The Long Run
- Encouragement For His Decisions
- Encouragement for Him at Home
- Other Encouragement

Remember that you can never tell you husband these two things too much:

1. *"I love you"*

2. *"I am proud of you"*

<u>Encouragement When he is Hurting</u>

- *"I love you no matter what"*

- *"I am here for you"*

- *"How can I serve you better?"*

- *"I love you no matter what!"*

- *"I believe in you"*

- *"It going to be OK"*

- *"When push comes to shove, I will always choose you"*

- *"We can get through this together, you are not alone"*

- *"This too shall pass"*

- *"I know you are going through a rough time, when you are ready to talk; I will be here for you"*

- *"I fully support you"*

- *"Don't give up and don't give in - stand your ground and I support you 100%"*

- *"Would you like to talk?"*

- *"Tomorrow is a new day"*

Encouragement When he is Hurting

- *"I don't completely understand what you are feeling, but I love you no matter what"*

- *"Try to forget todays troubles, and focus on the blessings"*

- *"You are not a failure"*

- *"Do you need a hug?"*

- *"You are important to me"*

- *"God is in control"*

- *"I love you no matter what"*

Encouraging his Physical Attributes

- *"I love you no matter what"*

- *"You are so handsome"*

- *"I love that you work out and take care of your body"*

- *"You look great"*

- *"Will you wear that _____ that you look so good in?*

- *"You really look good in that outfit."*

- *"You smell good"*

- *"I love looking into your eyes"*

- *"I love watching you from across the room"*

- *"I love your laugh"*

- *"I love being seen in public with you"*

- *"When I think about you, it brings a smile to my face"*

- *"You have incredible eyes"*

- *"You are the most handsome man I have ever seen"*

- *"No one compares to you"*

Encouraging his Physical Attributes

- *"I love falling asleep in your arms"*

- *"You have an incredible smile"*

- *"I love waking up with you each morning"*

- *"You are good looking"*

- *"I love your hair"*

- *"I love you no matter what"*

- *"I love all of your perfect imperfections"*

Feel free to positively comment on other parts of his body.
You should know your husband well enough to know what
part to comment on and which parts to leave alone.   Be wise!
Remember that men can be incredibly sensitive about their
looks and body.

Encouragement for Him as a Father

- *"You are a great father"*

- *"You are doing a great job with the kids"*

- *"I love how you pour your life into our children"*

- *"Thank you for being such a positive influence for our family"*

- *"I want our boys to grow up just like you"*

- *Thank you for being such a great example for our children"*

- *"What would we do without you?"*

- *"You bring honor to our family"*

- *"I would not want anyone else to be the father of our children"*

- *"Thanks for being such a hard worker"*

- *"Thank you for making our family a priority"*

- *"Our children are a reflection of you"*

- *"You are a blessing to me and the kids"*

- *"You are a great example to other young fathers"*

- *"We make beautiful babies"*

Encouragement for Him as a Father

- *"Thank you for setting the example for our girls future husbands"*

- *"You are an incredibly hard worker - thank you"*

- *"I love watching you play with the kids"*

- *"Words cannot express how much I appreciate what you do for our family"*

- *"I love you no matter what"*

- *"You are a great leader"*

- *"Thanks for working so hard to provide for our family"*

Encouragement for Him as a Husband

- *"You are my handsome husband"*

- *"Thanks for asking me to marry you"*

- *"I love you"*

- *"You are my best friend"*

- *"I need you"*

- *"I want you"*

- *"Thank you for _____ "(you fill in the blank)*

- *"You are a great husband"*

- *"You make me a better woman"*

- *"You are so handsome"*

- *"You complete me"*

- *"I am a lucky dog!"*

- *"You are a blessing to me"*

- *"You make me want to be a better woman"*

- *"I am the luckiest woman in the world"*

Spiritual Encouragement for Him

- *"How can I pray for you?"*

- *"Let's pray together"*

- *"I praise God for you "*

- *"I've been praying for you"*

- *"When I pray to God, I thank Him for you"*

- *"I praise God for bringing you into my life"*

- *'I love that the fruits of the spirit are evident in your life."*

- *"You are such a blessing to me"*

- *"I love how you use your skills and abilities to bless others"*

- *"Thank you for serving others"*

- *"It is so obvious that you love God"*

- *"Let's worship together as a family"*

- *"I have a new devotion book I would like us to use together"*

- *"I love you no matter what"*

- *"Thank you for being the spiritual leader of our family"*

General Encouragement for Him

- *"I love you"*

- *"You are so good looking"*

- *"Great job!"*

- *"I believe in you"*

- *"I trust you"*

- *"You are incredibly talented"*

- *"You can do it!"*

- *"I have confidence in you"*

- *"I love your positive **can do** attitude"*

- *"Have I told you lately how much I love you?"*

- *"No one compares to you"*

- *"You are an incredible man"*

- *"You can do anything you set your mind to"*

- *"You are so handsome"*

- *"I love you"*

- *"I am so proud of you"*

Encouragement by Time Together

- *"Would you like to go on a date?"*

- *"What would you like to do today?"*

- *"I have a surprise for you"*

- *"Here are some tickets for* _____ *"*

- *"Let's get away for the weekend"*

- *"I cannot wait to see you!"*

- *"You choose"* (dinner date, TV stations, music etc)

- *"You take the remote and pick something for us to watch"*

- *"I have hired a babysitter and we are going out this weekend"*

- *"Let's celebrate"*

- *"Let's go for a walk"*

- *"I have a song I want to sing to you"*

- *"I ordered your favorite take-out food, let's have a home date night"*

Encouragement by Time Together

- *"Let's grab a cup of coffee and talk"*

- *"I just love spending time with you"*

- *"Spending time with you is such a blessing"*

- *"Grab a blanket and let's go look at the stars and make a wish"*

- *"Let's go to_____ (fill in an event or thing he would like to do"*

Encouragement When he is Tired

- *"I love you no matter what"*

- *"I know you have had a tough day, let's get some takeout for dinner tonight."*

- *"Sit back and relax, I got this"*

- *"Let me watch the kids tonight and you enjoy some time to yourself"*

- *"How can I help you?"*

- *"I filled the tub with hot water - enjoy"*

- *"I got you some _____ "(fill in blank with his favorite comfort food)*

- *"Would you like a massage?"*

- *"Let me give you a big hug"*

- *"It will all look better after you get some rest"*

- *"What can I do to help?"*

- *"Thanks for being such a hard worker!"*

Encouragement for The Long Run

- *"I only want to walk through life with you by my side"*

- *"I want to grow old with you"*

- *"You are the only one for me"*

- *"I will never leave you nor forsake you"*

- *"Nothing can separate us"*

- *"We are ONE!"*

- *"I choose you"*

- *"We make a great team"*

- *"You are the only one for me"*

- *"You make life worth living"*

- *"I could not do this without you"*

- *"Thanks for being there for me"*

- *"When I am with you, all my troubles are far away"*

- *"When the going gets tough, I will be there right by your side"*

- *"If I had to do it all over again, I would choose you"*

Encouragement for His Decisions

- *"I love you no matter what"*

- *"I love how you handled that situation"*

- *"You were right"*

- *"I trust you with our finances"*

- *"I appreciate that you always have our best interests in mind"*

- *"That must have been really hard for you do say - thank you for having the courage to speak up"*

- *"Thank you for making wise decisions"*

- *"I know we can always trust you"*

- *"Thank you for sweating the small details"*

- *"What do you think about _____"*

- *"I could use some advice"*

- *"Thank you for your honesty"*

- *"Thank you for leading our family with confidence"*

- *"Thank you for protecting us:*

Encouragement for Him at Home

- *"Thank you for fixing the little things"*

- *"Thanks for completing the honey do list"*

- *"That meal you cooked was fantastic"*

- *"Thank you for planning out the meals each week"*

- *"You are an incredible cook"*

- *"Your garden is so nice, you have a real green thumb"*

- *"I love how you make the yard and landscaping look so good"*

- *"I cannot wait to come home each day and see you"*

- *"Thank you for opening our home to bless others"*

- *"Thank you for taking care of the cooking and cleaning - you are such a blessing to me and our family"*

- *"Thanks for being such a handy man"*

- *"I don't know how we could get along without you"*

- *"Thank you for providing for us"*

- *"Thank you for doing the grocery shopping"*

- *"Thanks for _____ (fill in blank)"*

Other Encouragement

- *"I missed you, I am glad you a finally home"*

- *"When we are not together, I don't feel the same"*

- *"I love how disciplined you are"*

- *"You have been a great sibling to your brothers and sisters"*

- *"I am sorry for _____"*

- *"Will you forgive me for _____"*

- *"I forgive you"*

- *"You are very talented with _____"*

- *"I want you to pursue your dreams!"*

- *"How can I be a dream maker for you?"*

- *"I took care of that _____ that I know you do not like to do"*

- *"You are a great son to your parents"*

- *"I am very proud of the way you serve your parents"*

- *"I love how you continue to make your parents a priority in your life"*

- *"I love you no matter what"*

As with all the lists and suggestions in book, the things you need to say to your husband is not comprehensive. It is meant to be a thought starter and reminder of how you need to communicate with your husband.

I would encourage you to use this list and see how many of these sayings you can use over the course of a year. It goes without saying that you should be sincere and that this should not feel forced or contrived. You may be uncomfortable with some of these things, but he will appreciate your effort.

Remember - he is worth it!

Notes Page

Use the page to take notes and suggested actions or next steps.

Things he Needs to Read

In addition to the verbal communication you will have with your husband, you can also take the opportunity to work on your writing skills and creativity to encourage your husband.

Below are some suggestions.   I would encourage you to use all of the technology at your disposal to encourage your husband (cell phone, computer, tablet, apps, pen and paper etc.)

- A quick text in the morning after you get to work to say "hello - I love you"

- Text him throughout the day to tell how handsome he is and how much you miss him.

- Write him a "real" love letter or card and put in in the mail.   Take the time to buy a bunch of stamps.

- Invest in some nice personal stationary when you write him those notes.

- Send him a text while you are out running errands and just tell him you are thinking about him

- Send him an e-mail with a greeting card attached

Things He Needs to Read

- Leave little notes for him in following places :
    - On his pillow
    - In his car
    - In different draws around your house
    - In the refrigerator

- Use your social media to complement and praise your husband. Your Facebook, Twitter, Instagram etc. should resonate with your love and admiration for your husband. There should be no question as to who your best friend is.

- Send him a text or email everyday with a new way to say how much you love and appreciate him.

- Have the kids write him some "love notes" and surprise him when he comes home.

- Send him a text or email everyday with a new way to say how much you love and appreciate him.

- Use the mirror in your bathroom as your own "encouragement sketch pad" and leave him some messages.

You know your husband better than anyone, so take all of these ideas as suggestions and use the ones that you know will resonate with him.

Notes Page

Use the page to take notes and suggested actions or next steps.

Little Things You Need to Do

- A minimum of three kisses each day (in morning when you leave for work, when you get home, when you say good night). Remember this is just the minimum

- Hold his hand - at home, at church, on a date, on a walk etc.

- Run some of the errands for him

- Turn the coffee on in the morning (even if you do not drink coffee)

- Teach your daughters to love and respect their father - be a positive role model for them

- Pick up after yourself

- Pillow talk!

- Clean up your messes (both in the house and in the garage, basement or yard)

- Take care of yourself (exercise and stay fit - do not let your body go downhill)

Little Things You Need to Do

- Wash up, Clean Up, Fix Up (we men want to see our Brides fixed up and pretty)

- If you handle the money - take some time periodically to bring him up to speed on the finances

- Be responsible with your money and have a clear family budget

- Don't get carried away with hobbies (be considerate about how much time and money you invest in your hobbies)

- Pray together

- Pray with the whole family

- Worship together

- Serve others together

- Buy him some of his favorite comfort food

- If you have little children, help with bed time routines (bathing, brushing teeth, story time, getting dressed etc)

- Rub his - neck, feet, shoulders (whatever he enjoys)

Little Things You Need to Do

- Dress nicely for your husband (he really does not like the "sweat" shirt - she was just being polite when he said he liked it).

- Cook him a meal (breakfast, lunch or dinner) and then clean up the mess

- Breakfast in bed (and not just on Father's day)

- If you travel and are on the road a lot, invest in the technology so you can video conference with your husband through Skype or other application.

- Hugs are always a good physical reminder to your husband how much you love him. If you are not a "hugger", I would encourage you to become one! A hug is just a physical way of saying "I love you".

- Consciously smile when you look at your husband! A wonderful smile is better than a thousand words.

- Ask your friends and neighbors who have successful and growing marriages how they encourage their husband.

- If your mom did a good job of encouraging your dad, get some tips from her.

Notes Page

Use the page to take notes and suggested actions or next steps.

Investing in Your Husband

All of these suggestions will require an investment of your time and some of them will require an investment of your money.   I can almost guarantee that you will see a great "return on investment" by focusing on your husband.

My only caveat is that these investments should be from the heart and not driven by an act of contrition on your part.

First let's start with things you cannot forget:

- Do not forget your anniversary

- Do not forget his birthday

- Do no forget the kids birthdays

- Do not forget Valentine's Day

- Do not forget Father's day

- Do not forget other important events (games, shows, parties, gatherings, etc.)

Investing in Your Husband

Also, here are some things you typically **should NOT** buy for your husband (yes I recognize there will be some exceptions to these rules). Know your husband and what he likes and dislikes.

- Household appliances (e.g. Toaster, Blender, Vacuum)

- Tickets to **your** favorite event (e.g. Ice Skating)

- Utensils

- Towels or Sheets

- Dishes

- Furniture

Now how can you invest in your husband?

- Food! The way to a man's heart is typically through his stomach. Maybe not true for all men, but certainly true for the majority of us men.

Investing in Your Husband

- Get him a gift certificate for his favorite store

- Hire a lawn service to beautify the yard when he is too busy to get it done

- Give him the day off to enjoy some time for himself

- Learn a new recipe and cook him a complete meal

- Hire a babysitter on a regular basis so you can have time together without kids

- Make vacations a priority (you should consider this an investment and not a cost)

- If he travels for work- make the effort to go to the airport and meet him for a quick date

- Fill the house with love notes - leave them everywhere

- Take care of the yard

- Do the laundry

- Clean up the garage and or basement

Investing in Your Husband

- Put some money in an envelope and label it "mad money" and tell him to enjoy himself.

- Make out a calendar of events for the year and surprise him with all the time you are going to invest in him

- Make him a coupon book filled with different date ideas that he can redeem at any time

- Enroll him in a "Coffee Club" that will send him a new type of coffee once per month (you can also do this with other products as well)

- Clean and vacuum the house (especially the kitchen)

- Take the kids for the day (or the weekend) and give him some time to himself

- Support his hobbies and talents by giving him the time to enjoy and pursue them.

Investing in Your Husband

- Buy some books on marriage and family enrichment and study them yourself! Apply what you learn from these books in your marriage.

- Attend a women's conference at your local church or out of town (he will appreciate that you are trying to become a better Bride and mother)

- Create a "slush fund" to spend on him by putting money in a jar that you would normally spend on a cup of coffee. Do this for 30 days and you will have quite a bit of money to treat your husband.

This list could be endless, but the key point is that you need to understand what will resonate best with your husband and then make the investment in him. He will very much appreciate that thought and if you have made some wise choices, he will also appreciate the gift as well.

<u>Notes Page</u>

Use the page to take notes and suggested actions or next steps.

Spending Time With Your Husband

(Dating your Husband - it does not have to be expensive)

There is no better way to encourage your husband than spending time with him!

Below are a number of examples of ways to spend time with your husband. Some of them will require an investment (note I did not say cost) but many of them will only require you to be thoughtful and invest your time.

- Go for a walk!

- Go to a wedding together and repeat your vows along with the couple getting married

- Attend a local high school sports teams game (you don't even have to know anybody playing - pretend you are in high school again)

- Dance with your husband - you can do this at home or on a date.

- Watch the sunrise

Spending Time with Your Husband

- Watch the sunset

- Go on picnic

- Dinner and a movie

- Go to a carnival

- Learn to play tennis together

- Make it a Netflix night

- Progressive fast food date (Salad at Wendy's, French Fries at McDonalds, sandwich at Burger King, milkshake at Dairy Queen)

- Listen to some of his favorite music together

- Take him to a concert

- Buy him seasons tickets to his favorite sports team in your town (this way you have guaranteed number of dates for each year)

- Make a "wish" list together and try to accomplish one of the wishes.

Spending Time with Your Husband

- Attend a marriage enrichment seminar

- Get away for a long weekend together

- Break out the beach chairs in the living room and watch a fun beach movie

- Take him out dancing

- Go to a "pick your own" farm and pick some fruit

- If you don't know how to dance, sign up for dance lessons together

- Sit and drink a cup of coffee together in the morning (or at night)

- Fix a meal of her favorite foods (and clean up the mess)

- Surprise him at work with a lunch date

- Go for a hike in a national or state park

- Go play Frisbee

- Go thrift store shopping and look to buy a gift for each other under $10

Spending Time with Your Husband

- Put a blanket out in the yard and look at the stars

- Find a new recipe and cook it together

- Go to a local museum

- Go to yard/garage sales on a Saturday morning

- Take a tour of a local company

- Start a garden

- Book a cruise

- Go to a trampoline park for the day

- Go buy a kite on a windy day and have some fun

- Bowling anyone?

- Join the local gym or YMCA and exercise together

- Go to the farmers market

- Visit antique stores

- Attend a local festival

- Go to the zoo

- Go shopping for a new car (even if you don't need one)

Spending Time with Your Husband

- Try French Fries from all the local fast food joints and vote on your favorite

- Work on a home project together

- Learn a new language together

- Go to a water park together

- Go to a local park on a partly cloudy day and talk about the different shapes of the clouds

- Play hide and seek in the house

- Go to a stable and learn to ride horses

- Break out Monopoly (or other board game)

- Spend the evening watching hilarious YouTube videos

- Go swinging at the playground

- Pretend you are in middle school again and go skating

- During the holidays, go look at houses that are decorated

Spending Time with Your Husband

- Find a waterfall near you and drive or hike to it

- Go to the circus

- Rent a canoe

- Head to the local coffee shop and just chill

- Go white water rafting

- Wake up early and go to the local bakery or doughnut shop and get something fresh

- Find a "dollar" theater and watch movies all day

- Go to the mall food court (try a least one new thing)

- Get some ice cream at Dairy Queen

- Go to Trip Advisor and find some cool things to do around your home that you probably never heard of.

- Volunteer together at a food bank for the day

- Help build a home with Habitat for Humanity

- Go to a play at the local high school or college

Spending Time with Your Husband

- Go to YELP/Urban Spoon or other internet sight and find a new restaurant to try.

- Put a bunch of these date ideas in a bag and have him pick one.

- Pack a suitcase for him and pick him up at work for a surprise weekend away

- Watch some of his favorite TV shows with her

- Grab a blanket and snuggle on the couch

- If you have a fire place, have dinner in front of the fire

- Find a drive- in movie theater

- Dinner and a Redbox movie

- Go to a comedy club

- Jump in the car and take a drive (doesn't matter where)

- If you live in the city, jump on the Train and take a ride

- Rent a cabin in the woods for the weekend

Spending Time with Your Husband

- Wake up at 2am and head to a local 24 hour restaurant (Waffle House, Ihop, Denny's etc.)

- Give your husband a massage along with some of his favorite snack foods.

- Pop some popcorn, grab a pen and paper and make out your bucket list together

- Put together a puzzle

- Learn to play golf together

- Enroll in some community classes together

- Learn a new hobby you can both enjoy (like photography)

- Go rappelling

- Manicure and pedicure together

- Karaoke anyone?

- Study the Song of Solomon together

Spending Time with Your Husband

- Enjoy each season outdoors with different activities no matter how hot or cold

- Rake a huge pile of leaves and then jump into it

- Who said Disney was just for kids

- Rent a condo for the week and just enjoy each other's company (at the beach or in the mountains)

- Go backpacking or camping

- Go to your Alma Mater and stroll the campus

- Break out the video games and pizza and make a night of it.

- Go skeet shooting

- Nerf gun war (whoever wins cooks dinner)

- Visit the humane society and pet the animals

- Grab a line and go fishing

- Wander around Walmart

- Make s'mores over a fire (or in the microwave)

Spending Time with Your Husband

- Bake some cookies or a cake together

- Get massages together at the spa

- Go to an auction

- Have a "staycation" and do all the touristy stuff in your town

- Go watch fireworks

- Run through a field of wildflowers together

- Take a nap together

- Ask him what he would like to do and then go do it

This was obviously not a complete list of all the different things you can do to spend time with you husband, but it would certainly keep you busy for quite a while. The main point is that you should be spending both quality and quantity time with your husband. I encourage you to be creative and talk to your friends and neighbors about different date ideas and how to spend time with your husband.

Finally - one of the things you will want to strive for is to have at least one date night per week. One weekend away two to three times each year, and a full week away every 2-3 years.

Notes Page

Use the page to take notes and suggested actions or next steps.

Encouraging Quotes

There is only one way to avoid criticism: do nothing, say nothing, and be nothing. *–Aristotle*

Believe you can and you're halfway there. *–Theodore Roosevelt*

Winning isn't everything, but wanting to win is. *–Vince Lombardi*

"Never consider the possibility of failure; as long as you persist, you will be successful." - Brian Tracy

Fall seven times, stand up eight. *~Japanese Proverb*

Few things can help an individual more than to place responsibility on him, and to let him know that you trust him. *–Booker T. Washington*

"One has to remember that every failure can be a stepping stone to something better." Col. Harland Sanders

"

Encouraging Quotes

It is not the mountain we conquer but ourselves.
Edmund Hillary

The best time to plant a tree was 20 years ago. The second best time is now. **Chinese Proverb**

"Never give up on what you really want to do. The person with big dreams is more powerful than one with all the facts." - **Unknown**

If the wind will not serve, take to the oars. - **Latin Proverb**

*An unexamined life is not worth living. –***Socrates**

When you encourage others, you in the process are encouraged because you're making a commitment and difference in that person's life. Encouragement really does make a difference. **Zig Ziglar**

*You can't fall if you don't climb. But there's no joy in living your whole life on the ground. –***Unknown**

''Age is no barrier. It's a limitation you put on your mind.'' - **Jackie Joyner-Kersee**

Do what you can, where you are, with what you have. – **Teddy Roosevelt**

Encouraging Quotes

A word of encouragement from a teacher to a child can change a life. A word of encouragement from a spouse can save a marriage. A word of encouragement from a leader can inspire a person to reach her potential. **John C. Maxwell**

Nothing is impossible, the word itself says, "I'm possible!" **–Audrey Hepburn**

Nine tenths of education is encouragement.
Anatole France

If you're going through hell, keep going. **-Winston Churchill**

Either write something worth reading or do something worth writing. **–Benjamin Franklin**

I ask not for a lighter burden, but for broader shoulders.
-Jewish Proverb

"Everything will be OK in the end, if it's not OK, it's not the end.''
- Unknown

If you are a leader, you should never forget that everyone needs encouragement. And everyone who receives it - young or old, successful or less-than-successful, unknown or famous - is changed by it. **John C. Maxwell**

Encouraging Quotes

"When you come to the end of your rope, tie a knot and hang on." - **Franklin D. Roosevelt**

Twenty years from now you will be more disappointed by the things that you didn't do than by the ones you did do, so throw off the bowlines, sail away from safe harbor, catch the trade winds in your sails. Explore, Dream, Discover. – **Mark Twain**

If you can dream it, you can achieve it. – **Zig Ziglar**

If you want to lift yourself up, lift up someone else. –**Booker T. Washington**

"Don't be discouraged. It's often the last key in the bunch that opens the lock." - **Unknown**

Two roads diverged in a wood, and I – I took the one less traveled by, And that has made all the difference. –**Robert Frost**

A person who never made a mistake never tried anything new. – *Albert Einstein*

"

Encouraging Quotes

"Instruction does much, but encouragement everything."
— *Johann Wolfgang von Goethe*

"Instead of giving myself reasons why I can't, I give myself reasons why I can." - **Author Unknown**

Education costs money. But then so does ignorance. –**Sir Claus Moser**

You miss 100% of the shots you don't take. –**Wayne Gretzky**

Whether you think you can or you think you can't, you're right. – **Henry Ford**

A bend in the road is not the end of the road... unless you fail to make the turn. - **Unknown**

Life is 10% what happens to me and 90% of how I react to it. – **Charles Swindoll**

Remember no one can make you feel inferior without your consent. – **Eleanor Roosevelt**

Encouraging Quotes

"I don't regret the things I've done, I regret the things I didn't do when I had the chance." – **Unknown**

You can never cross the ocean until you have the courage to lose sight of the shore. –**Christopher Columbus**

When it is dark enough, you can see the stars.
Ralph Waldo Emerson

"In order to succeed, your desire for success should be greater than your fear of failure." – **Bill Cosby**

The difficulties of life are intended to make us better, not bitter.
Unknown

"The pessimist sees difficulty in every opportunity. The optimist sees opportunity in every difficulty" - **Winston Churchill**

"I'd rather be a failure at something I love than a success at something I hate." - **George Burns**

I didn't fail the test. I just found 100 ways to do it wrong. –
Benjamin Franklin

Encouraging Quotes

People often say that motivation doesn't last. Well, neither does bathing. That's why we recommend it daily. *–**Zig Ziglar***

It does not matter how slowly you go as long as you do not stop. – ***Confucius***

"You may not realize it when it happens, but a kick in the teeth may be the best thing in the world for you." **Walt Disney**

It's not the years in your life that count. It's the life in your years. – **Abraham Lincoln**

"When you feel like giving up, remember why you held on for so long in the first place." - ***Unknown***

"Life is short, live it. Love is rare, grab it. Anger is bad, dump it. Fear is awful, face it. Memories are sweet, cherish it." – ***Unknown***

"Character cannot be developed in ease and quiet. Only through experience of trial and suffering can the soul be strengthened, ambition inspired, and success achieved."- **Helen Keller**

Rock bottom is good solid ground, and a dead end street is just a place to turn around. *-**Buddy Buie and J.R. Cobb***

Encouraging Quotes

Do you give as much energy to your dreams as you do to your fears?
Unknown

Life is short, fragile and does not wait for anyone. There will NEVER be a perfect time to pursue your dreams & goals.
Unknown

Don't say you don't have enough time. You have exactly the same number of hours per day that were given to Helen Keller, Bill Gates, Michelangelo, Mother Teresa, Leonardo da Vinci, Thomas Jefferson, and Albert Einstein. **Unknown**

Even the greatest was once a beginner. Don't be afraid to take that first step. **Unknown**

"The first to apologize is the bravest. The first to forgive is the strongest. The first to forget is the happiest."
Unknown

"Never get tired of doing little things for your spouse. Sometimes those little things occupy the biggest part of their heart." **Unknown**

"There is nothing more admirable than two people who see eye-to-eye keeping house as man and wife, confounding their enemies, and delighting their friends." **Homer**

Encouraging Quotes

"When I am with you, the only place I want to be is closer." **Unknown**

"Marriage succeeds only as lifetime commitment with no escape clauses." **Dr. James Dobson**

"A wise physician once said, 'The best medicine for humans is love.' Someone asked, 'What if it doesn't work?' He smiled and answered, 'Increase the dose'." **Unknown**

"I want a marriage more beautiful than my wedding." **Unknown**

"Marriage is like a fine wine, if tended properly, it just gets better with age." **Unknown**

"Don't marry the person you think you can live with; marry only the individual you think you can't live without."-**James C. Dobson**

"Love is just a word until someone comes along and gives it meaning." **Unknown**

"

Encouraging Quotes

When one door closes another door opens; but we so often look so long and so regretfully upon the closed door, that we do not see the ones which open for us." - **Alexander Graham Bell**

A diamond is merely a lump of coal that did well under pressure." **Unknown**

Lean on each other's strengths. Forgive each other's weaknesses." **Unknown**

Encouraging Scripture

Matthew 11:28-30
"Come to Me, all who are weary and heavy-laden, and I will give you rest. Take My yoke upon you and learn from Me, for I am gentle and humble in heart, and you will find rest for your souls. For My yoke is easy and My burden is light."

Romans 8:28
And we know that God causes all things to work together for good to those who love God, to those who are called according to His purpose.

Ephesians 5:25
Husbands, love your wives, just as Christ also loved the church and gave Himself up for her,

1 Peter 5:7
Casting all your anxiety on Him, because He cares for you.

1 Thessalonians 5:9-11
For God has not destined us for wrath, but for obtaining salvation through our Lord Jesus Christ, who died for us, so that whether we are awake or asleep, we will live together with Him. Therefore encourage one another and build up one another, just as you also are doing.

Encouraging Scripture

2 Corinthians 4:16-18
Therefore we do not lose heart, but though our outer man is decaying, yet our inner man is being renewed day by day. For momentary, light affliction is producing for us an eternal weight of glory far beyond all comparison, while we look not at the things which are seen, but at the things which are not seen; for the things which are seen are temporal, but the things which are not seen are eternal.

2 Thessalonians 2:16-17
Now may our Lord Jesus Christ Himself and God our Father, who has loved us and given us eternal comfort and good hope by grace, comfort and strengthen your hearts in every good work and word.

2 Thessalonians 3:16
Now may the Lord of peace Himself continually grant you peace in every] circumstance. The Lord be with you all!

2 Timothy 1:7
For God has not given us a spirit of timidity, but of power and love and discipline.

Colossians 3:15
Let the peace of Christ rule in your hearts, to which indeed you were called in one body; and be thankful.

Encouraging Scripture

Deuteronomy 31:6
Be strong and courageous, do not be afraid or tremble at them, for the Lord your God is the one who goes with you. He will not fail you or forsake you."

Ephesians 4:2-3
with all humility and gentleness, with patience, showing tolerance for one another in love, being diligent to preserve the unity of the Spirit in the bond of peace.

Galatians 6:9
Let us not lose heart in doing good, for in due time we will reap if we do not grow weary.

Hebrews 10:25
not forsaking our own assembling together, as is the habit of some, but encouraging one another; and all the more as you see the day drawing near.
Hebrews 13:8
Jesus Christ is the same yesterday and today and forever.

Hebrews 6:18
 so that by two unchangeable things in which it is impossible for God to lie, we who have taken refuge would have strong encouragement to take hold of the hope set before us.

Encouraging Scripture

Isaiah 40:31
Yet those who wait for the Lord
Will gain new strength;
They will mount up with wings like eagles,
They will run and not get tired,
They will walk and not become weary.

Isaiah 41:10
'Do not fear, for I am with you;
Do not anxiously look about you, for I am your God.
I will strengthen you, surely I will help you,
Surely I will uphold you with My righteous right hand.'

Isaiah 41:13
"For I am the Lord your God, who upholds your right hand,
Who says to you, 'Do not fear, I will help you.'

James 1:2-4
Consider it all joy, my brethren, when you encounter various trials, knowing that the testing of your faith produces endurance. And let endurance have its perfect result, so that you may be perfect and complete, lacking in nothing.

John 14:27
Peace I leave with you; My peace I give to you; not as the world gives do I give to you. Do not let your heart be troubled, nor let it be fearful.

Encouraging Scripture

Jeremiah 29:11-14
For I know the plans that I have for you,' declares the Lord, 'plans for welfare and not for calamity to give you a future and a hope. Then you will call upon Me and come and pray to Me, and I will listen to you. You will seek Me and find Me when you search for Me with all your heart. I will be found by you,' declares the Lord, 'and I will restore your fortunes and will gather you from all the nations and from all the places where I have driven you,' declares the Lord, 'and I will bring you back to the place from where I sent you into exile.'

John 14:1-3
"Do not let your heart be troubled; believe in God, believe also in Me. In My Father's house are many dwelling places; if it were not so, I would have told you; for I go to prepare a place for you. If I go and prepare a place for you, I will come again and receive you to Myself, that where I am, there you may be also.

John 16:33
These things I have spoken to you, so that in Me you may have peace. In the world you have tribulation, but take courage; I have overcome the world."

Joshua 1:9
Have I not commanded you? Be strong and courageous! Do not tremble or be dismayed, for the Lord your God is with you wherever you go."

Encouraging Scripture

Mark 11:24
Therefore I say to you, all things for which you pray and ask, believe that you have received them, and they will be granted you.

1 Peter 4:8
Above all, keep fervent in your love for one another, because love covers a multitude of sins.

Philippians 4:13
I can do all things through Him who strengthens me.

Philippians 4:6-7
Be anxious for nothing, but in everything by prayer and supplication with thanksgiving let your requests be made known to God. And the peace of God, which surpasses all comprehension, will guard your hearts and your minds in Christ Jesus.

Romans 8:31
What then shall we say to these things? If God is for us, who is against us?

Proverbs 17:17
A friend loves at all times,
And a brother is born for adversity.

Encouraging Scripture

Proverbs 18:10
The name of the Lord is a strong tower;
The righteous runs into it and is safe.

Proverbs 3:5-6
Trust in the Lord with all your heart
And do not lean on your own understanding.
In all your ways acknowledge Him,
And He will make your paths straight.

Proverbs 30:5
Every word of God is tested;
He is a shield to those who take refuge in Him.

Psalm 118:14
The Lord is my strength and song,
And He has become my salvation.

Psalm 119:50
This is my comfort in my affliction,
That Your word has revived me.

Psalm 34:8
O taste and see that the Lord is good;
How blessed is the man who takes refuge in Him!

Encouraging Scripture

Psalm 16:5-8
The Lord is the portion of my inheritance and my cup;
You support my lot.
The lines have fallen to me in pleasant places;
Indeed, my heritage is beautiful to me.
I will bless the Lord who has counseled me;
Indeed, my mind instructs me in the night.
I have set the Lord continually before me;
Because He is at my right hand, I will not be shaken.

Psalm 18:32-36
The God who girds me with strength
And makes my way blameless?
He makes my feet like hinds' feet,
And sets me upon my high places.
He trains my hands for battle,
So that my arms can bend a bow of bronze.
You have also given me the shield of Your salvation,
And Your right hand upholds me;
And Your gentleness makes me great.
You enlarge my steps under me,
And my feet have not slipped.

Psalm 27:14
Wait for the Lord;
Be strong and let your heart take courage;
Yes, wait for the Lord.

Encouraging Scripture

Psalm 27:1
The Lord is my light and my salvation;
Whom shall I fear?
The Lord is the defense of my life;
Whom shall I dread?

Psalm 46:1-3
God is our refuge and strength,
A very present help in trouble.
Therefore we will not fear, though the earth should change
And though the mountains slip into the heart of the sea;
Though its waters roar and foam,
Though the mountains quake at its swelling pride. Selah.

Psalm 55:22
Cast your burden upon the Lord and He will sustain you;
He will never allow the righteous to be shaken.

Psalm 28:7
The Lord is my strength and my shield;
My heart trusts in Him, and I am helped;
Therefore my heart exults,
And with my song I shall thank Him.

Psalm 37:4
Delight yourself in the Lord;
And He will give you the desires of your heart.

Encouraging Scripture

Psalm 121:1-8
I will lift up my eyes to the mountains;
From where shall my help come?
My help comes from the Lord,
Who made heaven and earth.
He will not allow your foot to slip;
He who keeps you will not slumber.
Behold, He who keeps Israel
Will neither slumber nor sleep.
The Lord is your keeper;
The Lord is your shade on your right hand.
The sun will not smite you by day,
Nor the moon by night.
The Lord will protect you from all evil;
He will keep your soul.
The Lord will guard your going out and your coming in
From this time forth and forever.

Psalm 31:24
Be strong and let your heart take courage,
All you who hope in the Lord.

Romans 15:4-5
For whatever was written in earlier times was written for our
instruction, so that through perseverance and the
encouragement of the Scriptures we might have hope. Now
may the God who gives perseverance and encouragement
grant you to be of the same mind with one another according
to Christ Jesus,

Encouraging Scripture

Psalm 34:4
I sought the Lord, and He answered me,
And delivered me from all my fears.

Romans 5:1
Therefore, having been justified by faith, we have peace with
God through our Lord Jesus Christ,

Psalm 55:22
Cast your burden upon the Lord and He will sustain you;
He will never allow the righteous to be shaken.

Romans 15:13
Now may the God of hope fill you with all joy and peace in
believing, so that you will abound in hope by the power of the
Holy Spirit.

Romans 8:38-39
For I am convinced that neither death, nor life, nor angels, nor
principalities, nor things present, nor things to come, nor
powers, nor height, nor depth, nor any other created thing,
will be able to separate us from the love of God, which is in
Christ Jesus our Lord.

Other Resources

Below are some additional websites and resources you might want to consider and might prove helpful as you start to encourage your Bride.

I do not endorse any of these sites this is just a list for your convenience.

E-Greeting Cards - a great way to encourage your Husband

www.bluemountain.com
www.123greetings.com
www.americangreetings.com
www.smilebox.com

Marriage Retreats

www.winshape.org/Retreat/2.0/

Ideas for Dates and Places

www.tripadvisor.com
www.urbanspoon.com
www.yelp.com

On the next pages are some guys movies (in no particular order) that he will probably enjoy watching.

Great Guys Movies to Rent or Buy.

- Gladiator
- Terminator (1,2,3)
- Star Wars (any)
- Star Trek (any)
- The Longest Day
- Silverado
- Godfather (1,2, 3)
- Cool Hand Luke
- Dirty Harry
- Butch Cassidy and the Sundance Kid
- The Dirty Dozen
- Robocop
- The Right Stuff
- Kelly's Hero's
- Armageddon
- Brave Heart
- The Patriot
- Oceans 11, 12, 13
- Spartacus
- Planet of the Apes
- Bridge on the River Kwai
- Matrix
- Die Hard
- Rocky
- The Untouchables
- The Great Escape
- Bullitt
- The Shawshank Redemption
- Jaws
- Raiders of the Lost Ark
- The Sting
- Enemy of the State

Great Guy Movies to Rent or Buy

- Smokey and the Bandit
- All The Presidents Men
- Rudy
- Bull Durham
- Airplane
- Friday Night Lights
- Independence Day
- Forrest Gump
- Crimson Tide
- The Sum of All Fears
- Patriot Games
- The Hunt for Red October
- 61
- Catch Me if You Can
- Saving Private Ryan
- Top Gun
- Transformers
- Real Steel
- Bonnie & Clyde
- Mickey Blue Eyes
- The Bourne Identity
- The Bourne Supremacy
- The Bourne Ultimatum
- The Bourne Legacy
- 300
- Gran Torino
- Batman
- The Dark Knight
- The Italian Job
- Any James Bond Movie
- National Treasure (any)
- The Chronicles of Narnia (any)

Great Guy Movies to Rent or Buy

- Casablanca
- Gone in 60 Seconds
- Tombstone
- Platoon
- Taken
- True Grit
- Patton
- Lethal Weapon
- Red Dawn
- Glory
- Heart Break Ridge
- Lord of the Rings (any)
- The Hobbit (any)
- Air Force One
- Schindlers List
- Spiderman (any)
- We Were Soldiers
- Dances with Wolves
- High Plains Drifter
- X-men
- Captain America
- Hulk
- Sands of Iwo Jima
- Ben-Hur
- Avatar
- Midway
- Tora Tora Tora
- Miracle
- The Blind Side
- The Longest Yard
- Thor
- The Deer Hunter

Great Guy Movies to Rent or Buy

- The Magnificent Seven
- Father of the Bride
- Money ball
- Lone Survivor
- Chariots of Fire
- Unbroken
- Lawrence of Arabia
- Old Yeller
- Hitch
- How to Lose a Guy in 10 days
- Serendipity
- 12 Angry Men
- Inception
- Back to the Future
- We are Marshall
- North by Northwest
- Gravity
- The Prestige
- Das Boot
- The Lion King
- Amadeus
- Toy Story
- UP
- Heat
- Ironman
- The Avengers
- Groundhog Day
- The Princess Bride
- Stalag 17
- Monster Inc
- Jurassic Park
- A Christmas Story

Great Guy Movies to Rent or Buy

- The Alamo
- Big Jake
- Twister
- Men in Black
- Mission Impossible
- Saint
- Shrek

He may not like or enjoy all of these movies, but he will appreciate the effort you put forth to get him some movies he would like to watch. If you want to go the extra mile, then actually watch the movie with him.

In regards to sports:

You may not enjoy watching baseball, football, NASCAR, golf, or any sport for that matter. However, you can make it more enjoyable for yourself if you ask him to tell you about the players and personalities and in this way you may be able to engage and enjoy the event.

Suggested Weekly Schedule for Basic Encouragement

For those of you who do not know where to start and need an outline of what to do, below is a suggested weekly calendar for encouraging your husband. Remember, this is meant to be **very basic** and as your grow and mature, you should move beyond these basic ideas and timelines. Every man is different and unique, but they all crave love, respect and honor.

Monday -Friday

- Kiss him goodbye and tell him you love him
- Text message in the morning to encourage him
- Text message in the afternoon to encourage him
- At some point in the day, remind him how handsome he is and how lucky you are to be married to him
- Give him a kiss and hug when you get home (comment positively on how he looks)
- Remind him how important he is to you and to your family.
- Let him know that you respect him and appreciate his efforts to love and support the family
- Let him know you are praying for him
- Kiss him good night and give him a big hug

Saturday

- Continue with a kiss and hug to wake up
- If you are out running errands- send him an encouraging text message
- Continue with kiss and hug to wake up and kiss and hug when you go to bed
- Date night - have something fun planned
- Tell him how handsome he is
- Look for ways to thank him
- Tell him you love him multiple times today
- Continue with a kiss and hug when you go to bed

Sunday

- Continue with Kiss and hug to wake up
- Tell him how handsome he is
- Attend church and worship God together
- Take a nap together
- Fix him supper tonight and let him relax
- Tell him you love him multiple times today
- Continue with a kiss and hug when you go to bed

How to Discourage Your Husband

What does Proverbs say about discouraging your husband?

Proverbs 21:9
It is better to live in a corner of a roof
Than in a house shared with **a contentious** woman.

Proverbs 27:15
A constant dripping on a day of steady rain
And a **contentious** woman are alike;

Proverbs 21:19
It is better to live in a desert land
Than with a **contentious** and vexing woman.

Proverbs 25:24
It is better to live in a corner of the roof
Than in a house shared with a **contentious** woman.

Proverbs 11:22
As a ring of gold in a swine's snout
So *is* a beautiful woman who lacks discretion.

Proverbs 14:1
The wise woman builds her house,
But the foolish tears it down with her own hands.

I looked up the word **contentious** in the thesaurus and these are the different words that came up:

Argumentative
Quarrelsome
Antagonistic
Prickly
Touchy
Naysaying
Belligerent
Hot-blooded

In addition - here are the different words that came up for **contentious** from various bible translations:

NIV - quarrelsome
ESV - quarrelsome
King James - brawling
HCSB - nagging
TLB - crabby
MSG - nagging
The Voice - badgering
AMP - nagging, quarrelsome, *and* faultfinding

Nagging your husband is almost always a recipe for disaster!

Consider these verses and words as you think about your attitude and actions and how you can encourage your husband each and every day!

Final Thoughts

It is my hope and desire that you have found this book useful in your quest to encourage your husband. Now you have the opportunity to put your knowledge into action. It is not enough to know what to do, you must do it!!

Make the investment of your Time, Talents and Treasures and you will see the most incredible return in your relationship with your husband. He deserves a great woman and you have the opportunity to be that great woman for him.

Finally, if you are a mother, you will also be showing you daughter(s) how to treat their future husband and helping set the expectations for your son's future wife.

Blessings to you and your family!

Paul Beersdorf

I hope you enjoyed the book and it proves helpful in drawing you closer to your husband.

If you would like to provide any feedback, comments or thoughts, you can reach me at:

paulbeersdorf@gmail.com

---

www.ingramcontent.com/pod-product-compliance
Lightning Source LLC
Chambersburg PA
CBHW050550280326
41933CB00011B/1793